# TORONTO
## THE CITY OF NEIGHBOURHOODS

# TORONTO
## THE CITY OF NEIGHBOURHOODS

Marjorie Harris

Introduction by Harold Town

A Key Porter Book

McClelland and Stewart

**Canadian Cataloguing in Publication Data**

Harris, Marjorie.
    Toronto : the city of neighbourhoods

ISBN 0-7710-3988-3

1. Toronto (Ont.) — Description.   2. Toronto (Ont.)
— History.   3. Neighbourhood — Ontario — Toronto.
I. Title.

FC3097.52.H37 1984      971.3'541      C83-099321-5
F1059.5.T686A24 1984

Produced by Key Porter Books
59 Front Street East
Toronto, Ontario M5E 1B3

Published by McClelland and Stewart Ltd.
25 Hollinger Road
Toronto, Ontario M4B 3G2

Designed by Gerry Takeuchi
Typesetting by Q Composition
Printing by Everbest Printing Co. Ltd.

Printed and bound in Hong Kong

**Jacket Photograph Credits**
John de Visser (top right and bottom left)
Larry Morse (top left)
Richard Pierre (bottom right)

# TABLE OF CONTENTS

# INTRODUCTION
## By Harold Town

Neighbourhoods are the glue of cities, and best understood by the very young and the old. For a child, inside is today . . . outside is tomorrow . . . to the young, the neighbourhood is tomorrow, and for the very old, yesterday.

Children are the yeast of any neighbourhood; it is the place where they first probe the intricate world outside the rituals of family. Though in time the neighbourhood is both familiar and ordinary, it is still over-dimensioned, and becomes a workable abstraction, a useful part of the larger concept that extends the idea of family into the matrix of nationhood.

Near the end of his life, Arthur Meighen, a neighbour and ex-Prime Minister of Canada, though bent like the head of a cane, his feet seemingly velcroed to the sidewalk, took a daily constitutional along our street. Often he would stop, pat my daughter's head, and mutter a few words. She wasn't impressed. I just could not explain Meighen to her, or the fact that she was being touched by living history. Her neighbourhood was lively, and included Ronnie the postman, who crouched down and joked with her through what she called the "talking mail box". In time Ronnie made her assistant postie for the street, a job that ended abruptly when she was bitten by Captain, a jealous dog that followed Ronnie everywhere.

For the old, a neighbourhood can substitute for vanished friends and absent relatives, with the comfort of a community family in which the response to any emergency is swift and natural. In return the elderly, through memory, provide a continuum for a sense of place, with stories of how it used to be in the area.

Technically, a neighbourhood is a free association of people within casually fluctuating borders . . . a generalized and quite accidental community, with an unlimited membership. Though privately owned, all the houses, lanes, trees, lawns, and stores, become community property. The title to this mish-mash of urban stuff comes with oblique neigh-bourly accretions that stick to, and finally cover one, in the daily process of just walking by, in being there as a witness to the passage of the years. As the sailor owns the guiding beam of a lighthouse, so you own the friendly illumination of your neighbour's home, the insinuating odour of fresh cut grass rising from his lawn, and the splashing smile of his son as he tumbles from the house into a new day. He, in turn, shares your Christmas decorations glowing in the driving snow, the ambrosial wafting of chili sauce cooking in the kitchen, and the flickering of a pumpkin face hacked into a state of benign ghostliness by a miniature Michelangelo. In a neighbourhood, property is private but sensations are public.

Montaigne, in his essays, stated: "The same reason that makes us wrangle with a neighbour causes war between princes." Fortunately, the

negative factors of urban life, barking, befouling curs, top decibel ghetto blasters, writ-serving fence watchers, the penetrating stink of a local industry, streets made impassable by the parked cars of people who live everywhere else, are ground away by time. The bedlam and grit vanishes when the mind pulls back the curtain on a sweltering summer evening, cool air filtering down through trees as still as tomb stones, quenching the fire in seared pavement, and stiffening the tar rising in sidewalk cracks. Then, houses opened wide to the reviving night, letting the very essence, a secret centre of family life escape to float in the thick atmosphere, along with the moths bouncing off street lights.

Hoses hissing contrapuntally seemed to underscore the sporadic melody of verandah voices, sounds that silenced as a cigarette glowed or ice tinkled. Breaking off from a game of hide and seek, reluctant to give up the rich dark and return to parental light, kids scuffed their way home like escaped convicts returning to a chain gang. They glowed in the darkness from a browning day — a day that had seen them ride the back of the Belle Ewart wagon, pawing the wet shattered wood for shards of sucking ice, a day in which they had lost a friend, made a friend, traded a rusted skate key for half a yo-yo, and had played in illogical succession . . . buck-buck how many fingers up, tin can cricket, wall handball, street prison, baseball, circle jack knife, and football, with a pillow found in the garbage; a day in which they had pried nails out of a fence guarding a pear tree, preparatory to a night assault on fruit prematurely ripened by weeks of gustatory reconnoitering, and then had tried to make a substitute for alcohol out of kitchen vinegar, baking soda and salt stolen from a T.T.C. street bin.

They were trickling home from a sub-cosmos rarely seen by adults, for much of it existed under verandahs, in abandoned sheds, up lanes, on roofs, and behind fences. On the porches, dreams remained unfulfilled, but the kids had emptied theirs, slapping their own behinds as they cowboyed down the street, firing at imaginary Indians with a finger made dangerous only by dirt, or charging through the clouds over France, arms outstretched, shooting down the Red Baron, and then receiving the Victoria Cross from a Queen, who moments before, as Florence Nightingale, had bound their wounds.

A good neighbourhood is a sandwich, comprised of the young and the old, with a filling made from all the movers & shakers, the worried working dads and moms, the Mrs. and Mr. inbetweens whose real attention is somewhere else.

Unlike pens, glasses, or door keys, a neighbourhood is always just where you expect it to be. Change is anathema to a sense of neighbourhood, small change is acceptable, plant a tree, paint a house, repair a roof, put in a hedge or swimming pool. Fine! However, tear down the past and slap up a row of chi-chi rug brick, black metal tickle fence, canape size lawn, blister skylight roof, town house dinkies, and you have horizontal apartments, impersonal, blank as a banker's stare when you ask for money, just so much expensive neighbourhood rot.

Idiosyncratic behaviour, even eccentricity, is the essence of neighbourhood. Explain the man who dressed year in, year out, in funereal black, putting pink shingles on his house and matching flamingoes on the lawn, or the servant of God, who protected his walnut trees from boys and squirrels with the savagery of a full panzer division; or the corpulent lady much given to protesting that students smoked in the streets during lunch hour, parading her anger with the bottom of her skirt caught in the top of her voluminous drawers.

My favourite memories are of Barbara Cody, the widow of Canon Cody, and a next door neighbour for twenty years. She was thin as tissue paper, her teeth clicked and she conducted all conversation in the peripatetic mode; you either ran after her, walked with her, or just shouted at a distance; she was as swift as a spring trout, and much harder to catch. Sleep was her enemy; most nights she was still working past two in her second floor office at the back, darting about, filing papers in cardboard cartons. Her civic sense was immense – she served on committees, chaired meetings; whipping out of her driveway like Stirling Moss, she hurtled from one activity to another. No car seemed to last her more than two months . . . after she left one in the driveway it would tremble, leak fluid, and sort of whimper like a gut broke horse. Once I watched her make a complete circle in a four-way intersection. Fearing for her safety I mentioned the multiple infraction of law and good sense, she replied, "I was perfectly safe, for I had my hand out." She was a splendid menace! In between keeping the books devoted to her charitable contributions, she conducted a vast correspondence with converted Christians in India and the outposts, found time at her own cost to plant flowers in the mangy park at the end of the street, walk her dog, visit the sick, give innumerable teas, and fight me any time I tried to help her lift something twice her weight. On the eve of Canada's birthday in 1967, I caught her teetering on a decrepit step ladder, with a hammer that once must have belonged to Thor, trying to affix our flag to the tree out front. I had to plead, cajole and beg her to the ground, only to have her give me enough instructions once I took her place to cover the building of an office tower.

She was nudging eighty at this juncture, and seemed if anything to be speeding up: when tired, I thought of her, she was a psychic amphetamine and I loved her.

Every neighbourhood needs such a presence, for it is a billboard of hope, an advertisement for old age as passion and just plain doing – a blazing hurray for life after the first wrinkle, and a fist in the face of time.

The soul of an apartment building is hidden, even furtive and fearful; it is evinced only in sporadic elevator good-mornings, and the highly limited eccentricities of balcony decor. The doormen change as often as socks at a gymnasium, and there is no antidote for drunken parties, pounding rock racket and cigar smoke in the hall. Neighbourhoods give one time to really comprehend the residents; the way a man cuts his grass or trims a hedge is an arboreal Rorschach test . . . there are slashers and hackers, and those that tickle, pat, and beg grass into a condition that is something like broadloom, and the bumblers who fall over the rake, talk to everyone going by, accidentally snip the head of the roses, and after eight hours of strenuous fumble, leave the lawn looking as if it had just suffered an Argo scrimmage.

However, a neighbourhood is larger than the sum of its parts. It is more a feeling than a fact, a history without a designated recorder, and a benign and informal force. When someone dies there is a sense of loss, if a child is born, celebration. Quite simply, a neighbourhood as living beats a numbered cell in a cement bee hive. Without neighbourhoods cities are soulless mounds dedicated to commerce, a job site for the affluent, and a prison for the poor.

Though the adhesive of cities, neighbourhoods become blocks in the foundation of a nation.

# YORKVILLE/THE ANNEX

Trinity College in 1928. This building, which was erected in 1851 and has since been demolished, was the inspiration for some of the finest buildings on the University of Toronto campus.

(*Opposite page*) Some of the most attractive and imaginative 19th-century homes in the city are found in the Yorkville-Annex area. Most of the exteriors are intact, even though renovations have gone on inside. This Victorian vision of solidity, with elaborate sandstone carving and turret, is a good example of the size and spaciousness of many of these houses.

Two urban villages in the classic sense: they share a main street – Bloor – where commerce is conducted in everything from haute couture to bargain-basement specials. All the accoutrements for a rich and satisfying cultural life are here as well. Galleries and restaurants have been well-established for over two decades. Gracious churches, small parks and mansionettes create an exquisitely self-contained district. From Yonge Street to Bathurst in the west, Bloor to the railroad tracks on the north, these two areas live amiably side by side, divided only by Avenue Road.

Both neighbourhoods have resisted the outside pressure to raze graceful streetscapes for giant salt-boxes or permit expressways to rip through this leafy enclave so close to downtown. In such battles both demonstrate their long and honourable histories of independence.

The Annex, so called because it was annexed to the city in 1887 when most of it was lush countryside, became an escape from the vapours of the city for many of the Establishment families. The Gooderhams built their mansion in 1889 at the corner of St. George and Bloor, in the Romanesque style of the time. It set the tone for the wealthy WASPs who followed, and survives today as the prestigious York Club. Where the rich lived, those who served them followed, and workers' houses, narrow brick rows with mansard roofs, sprouted up on tiny streets such as Tranby and Boswell. It was all very Anglo-Saxon until after the Second World War when Hungarians, Italians and Ukrainians settled in to give it a rich ethnic flavour.

On Bloor, from Avenue Road to Spadina, there is a surprising variety of fast food outlets; further west, small independent shops and restaurants reflect the real life of the people who live in the streets behind. Greengrocers, hardware stores and cafes are daily meeting places for professors, painters, poets and students who are part of the lively mix. The West Annex, running from Spadina, has a happy tradition of neighbours knowing and helping one another, of block parties and yard sales. They reflect a feisty determination to keep things just the way they are.

Yorkville's history is much more turbulent. Joseph Bloor founded the village in 1830. Breweries and brickmaking were the two main industries. People were attracted to the dancing and parties at the Red Lion Inn (now demolished) at Yonge and Bloor. Since those days, constant activity and change have been very

Two views of the wide variety of styles in the district. The ladies on the right are sitting in the sun outside a Yorkville boutique. The women above are waiting to get into Honest Ed's for the twelve o'clock opening specials. This is one of the largest discount emporiums in the city, and people line up for hours to take advantage of the bargains.

much a part of the spirit of Yorkville. In the middle part of this century, artists were attracted to it because of the wonderful old houses. Albert Franck, among the most notable, spent a lifetime painting the original houses of his neighbourhood.

In the mid-1960s, hippies took over Yorkville Avenue attracting thousands of curiosity seekers to gaze at their antics. The street became celebrated among the young, and notorious to their elders. Toronto's very first coffee houses and clubs were here. The dingy cellars where Gordon Lightfoot, Joni Mitchell and Neil Young once sang have given way to extravagant restorations and elegant shops. The Yorkville of today reflects the opulence of Toronto. Those who make their fortunes in the downtown core come here to spend their money in this dazzling playground.

(*Previous pages*) Yorkville Avenue is one of Toronto's truly glamorous streets. The narrow, elegant 19th-century row houses have been converted into boutiques and galleries displaying an astonishing variety of wares. Behind them stands Hazelton Lanes, a shopping and apartment complex, one of the most successful of its kind in the city.

This stretch of Bloor Street in the West Annex is the main centre for Hungarian restaurants and shops. It also has the many cafes, record and book stores that serve as meeting places for the students and artists who live nearby. On a warm summer evening this can be one of the busiest corners downtown.

Back in the 1960s, Yorkville was the first area in the city where streetside dining became an accepted practice. On any fine day you can see outdoor cafes jammed with people-watchers sipping a glass of wine and eating the latest culinary fad. This is especially true in Yorkville where following the current fashion is a must.

# THE BEACHES

In 1916, the Beach, as it was then called, lured just as many people to take a dip on a hot day as it does now.

(*Opposite page*) The Beaches is famous for its sports and sporting heroes. Ted Reeve was so revered as a football player, later a sports writer, that they named an arena after him. The playing fields, such as this one, are in an idyllic setting, under beautiful old willow trees right next to the lake with its cooling breezes.

(*Overleaf*) Kew Beach with its adjacent park and the boardwalk is situated in one of the most felicitous spots in the city. Except for the intrusion of the CN Tower in the background, it's hard to believe this is close to downtown.

The Beaches is a rarity in Toronto: a neighbourhood with complete access to the waterfront. The boardwalk, the parks and the houses that border Lake Ontario have created one of the most relaxed areas in the city. No subway here, but the long stretch of the Queen Street car takes you into the city's earliest summer retreat. Going to the Beach (as old-timers call it) is still like escaping away from the city. So distinctive is the quality of The Beaches, as it was officially named in 1932, that it has eschewed the highrises that threaten so many of Toronto's neighbourhoods. This is and always has been an Anglo-Saxon bailiwick, much turned in upon itself, from its mores to its community institutions such as the Balmy Beach Canoe Club.

The area from Woodbine to the west over to Victoria Park and from the lake to Gerrard Street with Queen as its main street, is very much like a small, quiet town. Queen Street by contrast reveals a tremendous variety of antique and junque stores, health food emporia, good second-hand bookstores and an increasing number of good restaurants, cafes and some very British pubs.

The first settlers moved in around 1835. By 1865, the community began at a tollgate on Woodbine and Kingston Road. It was mostly simple farmland. The summer cottagers eventually winterized their homes and made them into permanent residences. Year-round settlement was abetted by the Toronto Street Railway which opened in the 1890s. The magnet for this shady haunt was a small amusement park, Scarborough Beach Park, which was torn down in 1926. Some of the very old Beach people feel that's when the real spirit left the community. Memories of Old England persist not only in the owners but in the houses they built: mock tudor half-timbering; even a new townhouse development has been created to look like the main street of an English village.

Athleticism is rampant in The Beaches. You have to watch for bikers, joggers, ropeskippers and Tai Chi experts on a simple stroll along the eight thousand feet of boardwalk by the water's edge. Recently, pollution has affected swimming in the lake but that has not discouraged the professional sunbathers. To be true Beach, you have to have a tan. And look fit.

In the 1960s, newcomers swamped The Beaches, upsetting the more stolid locals. They worried about upgraded houses and rising taxes, and about lowering the stock of rental properties. But it brought a whole new life to the drabness of Queen Street.

(*Above*) The streets south of Queen run straight down to the lake. Each one has a vista and some of the most interesting houses in the neighbourhood. It's a marvellous place to take a walk.

(*Opposite page*) During the summer, yard sales are a common sight all over Toronto. This one is being held outside a house with mock tudor facing, one of the many styles of architecture of The Beaches.

These young people were attracted as much by the green space as they were by the quirky nature of the old houses. There is more park per person than anywhere else in the city. There is also the highest concentration of old people outside Victoria B.C. and they are well serviced by a very caring community.

The Beaches is different from other neighbourhoods. It's a summer community that turned into a way of life. It is one of the friendliest neighbourhoods for visitors. But to really participate you have to live there for a long, long time.

The shops on this thoroughfare are
not concentrated in one area as they
are in most other neighbourhoods.
They are strung out all along the street
in the district. Fancy greengrocers,
toy shops and cafes are cheek-by-jowl
with dry cleaners, drug stores and
second-hand shops from an earlier,
more humble period.

One of the delights of The Beaches is
the eccentric nature of the architecture. It ranges from California Spanish
to Victorian whimsies such as this
enchanting house. The wide verandah
commands a splendid view of the lake.

# ST. CLAIR WEST

In 1938, St. Clair West was lined with small, mainly Anglo-Saxon-owned businesses.

(*Opposite page*) Westclair Village is chock-a-block with Italian businesses that range from jewellers, shoe and clothing stores, travel agencies to, of course, lots of good restaurants.

In July 1982, Italy won the World Cup of Soccer. On the night of the victory, Toronto's 500,000 Italians took to the streets around St. Clair and Dufferin waving green, white and red flags. It turned Westclair Village into one of the most glorious parties the city has ever seen. Ecstatic citizens came to celebrate in the part of the city that reflects an Italian home away from Italy.

The commerce of Westclair is conducted almost entirely in Italian. Almost all of the shops are owned by Italians. They offer the snappiest of new shoes in the brightest of colours, the latest in Italian fashions. In the food department, charming little cafes – called *tavola calda* by the locals – dish out veal and hot sausage sandwiches, and gelateria are open to the street dispensing the special Italian ices in a wondrous variety of flavours. Everywhere you hear the sound of CHIN radio.

Prospect Cemetery in the middle of the district goes back to 1826, and now resembles a graveyard more European than any other in the city. Photographs, plastic flowers and constant attention make it an almost cheerful place. Names on markers, however, reflect the earlier history of the neighbourhood. From the 1930s and 40s, the names are English and Jewish. This part of town was considered to be in the hinterlands in those days. Outdoor plumbing predominated, fish and chip shops and ramshackle second-hand stores made up the main part of the street scene. During this period, solid two-storey brick houses were being built. The oldest churches went back to the 1850s, giving the district a patina of continuity.

By the 1950s, the original Little Italy down at College and Spadina was thriving. Those who were on their way up moved north to St. Clair; the unattractive street started to hum to a slightly racier tune. Ten years later, Westclair was the centre of Italian merchandising for the whole city. By the 1970s, the confidence of the community exuded from every shop. In 1976, at Dufferin and Lawrence, Villa Colombo, a senior citizens' home opened, and Columbus Centre, a recreation, cultural and social services centre followed. They were built with millions of dollars raised by Italian-Canadians. Old and new immigrants (those who came before World War II and those who came after) pulled together. As labourers, they had practically built the city. Now their own buildings stand as a symbol of their enormous achievements.

(*Previous pages*) A bird's eye view of one of the most high-spirited parties Toronto has ever seen. When Italy won the World Cup of Soccer, St. Clair West was host to a seven-day, round-the-clock celebration.

The street itself holds such a wealth of attractions that even the most prosperous Italian-Canadians who have moved on to mansions in the suburbs come back every weekend. They return to play bocci and kick around a soccer ball in Earlscourt park, shop for real Italian produce and socialize with their family and friends and friends of family. Everyone in Little Italy on the weekend is a *paesano*, even if they don't happen to be Italian. It's that kind of neighbourhood.

(*Opposite page*) The Toronto Public Library system reflects the city's multicultural character. Neighbourhoods that have a strong ethnic mix carry books in the dominant languages spoken. These men are reading some of the five Italian-language journals that are published in Toronto.

(*Above*) Travelling through the neighbourhoods is a lot of fun if you go by streetcar, as you can along St. Clair West. You can see a lot more of what the city has to offer and you are likely to be tempted into hopping on and off to shop and browse.

Tightly-knit Italian families enjoy all major occasions together. In this case three generations of one family gather on their front porch to watch a religious procession from the local parish.

One of the joys of many Toronto
neighbourhoods is that there are lots
of wine bars. None are more cheerful
or welcoming than those on Westclair.
Italians come from everywhere in the
city and environs to enjoy them, especially on weekends.

# THE DANFORTH

In 1908, the Danforth area was annexed to Toronto, and this is what the new road looked like. It was not until 1912 that it was paved and linked up with Bloor and Sherbourne. Before this it was known as the muddy Danforth and it's easy to see why.

(*Opposite page*) Sunkist fruit market is probably the best-known in the city. It began in 1929 and is still run by members of the Comella family. They started the tradition of Danforth markets staying open all night.

If you close your eyes as you cross over the Prince Edward Viaduct to the Danforth, you might, just for a moment, feel you were in Athens. The smell of lamb broiling on a spit, the sound of Greek as the language of business, bouzouki clubs, the all-night fruit markets give the street an underlying Hellenic flavour.

The round-the-clock action now belies the fact that in the 1950s it was a repository of used-car lots, or that back in 1918 when the viaduct was completed, it was considered a politicians' folly: a bridge to nowhere. The largely Anglo-Saxon working-class area with its market gardens, brick factories and roadhouses was then considered a backwater.

With the advent of the viaduct, the Danforth was no longer cut off from the city by its natural boundary of the Don Valley. It prospered. So rapidly, in fact, that it has one of the highest commercial densities in the city. Everything could be bought and sold on the Danforth from cars and furniture, new and used, to mysterious herbal remedies. Discount merchandisers on tiny, narrow lots jammed into the six-mile-long street made it into a carnival of commercial vulgarity. The area, bounded by the Don Valley, Woodbine Avenue to the east, Gerrard to the south and several blocks north of Danforth Avenue, was the lower-middle-class suburb of Toronto. A place on the way up for those escaping from Cabbagetown. It stayed that way until the 1950s. Then Anglo-Saxons in the area started retreating to the suburbs. Italians moved in, followed, in the 1960s, by the largest concentration of Greeks in the city.

The street was named for Asa Danforth who, in 1799, cut the road we know as Queen Street. The area that includes Danforth was annexed to the city in 1884. It was nothing more than a dusty country road at the time. But Captain George Playter, a Loyalist, was granted five hundred acres of land in 1793. By the 1860s, Playter Estates became a suburb elegant enough to rival Rosedale which it faced across the Don River. By 1884, developers had started to lay out subdivisions in what had been orchards, dairy and market farms. In the early part of this century, churches and schools opened to serve the British immigrants who filled the district.

Today the population is still largely Anglo-Saxon in spite of the huge influx of Italians and Greeks. The tendency has been that when the Greeks integrate, they troop off to the suburbs to live. This in turn leaves room for the children of the Anglos who earlier

(*Above*) Playter Estates was home to the first settlers in the district. This home which was built in the 1870s by William Playter, a market gardener, stands on the site of the original crown grant. The stone porch and fence were additions to the original farmhouse.

(*Opposite page*) This magnificent Renaissance structure, Holy Name Church, was built in 1926. It was the first Roman Catholic church on the Danforth. The church's best-known alumnus is world-famous singer Lois Marshall who was a member of the choir during the 1940s.

fled the district, to return to the Danforth's solid old brick houses. With them come the inevitable renovations. You see them most notably on the streets of Riverdale around Withrow Park, and north of the Danforth on Playter Estates.

But the Greek ambiance remains in the commerce of Danforth Avenue, especially between Broadview and Pape. They are the good humoured neighbours of some of the oldest shops such as the Georgina Tea Room (1918) and Thuna Herbalists (1923) which are still going strong. It is this kind of juxtaposition that makes the Danforth such a dynamic neighbourhood.

A gala Italian wedding on the Danforth. The first Catholic church was erected by the Irish. The Italians, who began to arrive after World War II, built their own church, St. Catherine of Siena, in 1966.

Though Toronto had lots of fish and chip shops, the first real fresh fish market was established on the Danforth in 1915. The original, Chambers, is still a family-run business. In the 1960s, the Greeks opened up many more like this gaily decorated store.

(*Overleaf*) Greek restaurants such as this one are a common sight along the Danforth. In warm weather, all these places are packed, not just with locals but with people from every part of the city.

# CHINATOWN

A small section of the old Chinatown on Elizabeth Street in 1937. In the 1920s, clusters of Chinese shops opened up in this area which was known as The Ward and until then had been essentially a Jewish community.

(*Opposite page*) Sunday is the traditional market day in Chinatown. All the shops are open and people come from all over the city to buy the exotic produce available at the myriad greengrocers that jam the area.

Every city worthy of being called cosmopolitan has a Chinatown. Toronto's just happens to be the third largest in North America after San Francisco and New York. It is no less exotic than the others and is a touchstone to the changing nature of Toronto's neighbourhoods. Chinatown is crucial to more than 200,000 local citizens of Chinese extraction. But, it has also become part of the occidental way of life. A trip to Dundas Street for herbs and vegetables found only in this cluttered district is a necessity for any urban gourmet.

Toronto has two Chinatowns, old and new. The old Chinatown began with one person, Sam Ching. He started a laundry at 9 Adelaide St. W. in 1878. Other businesses opened up around him, but a real neighbourhood didn't take shape until the Chinese located behind City Hall at Elizabeth and Dundas. By sheer determination and hard work, the close-knit families bought houses all through the district. Eventually they had their own clubs, casinos, operas and theatres. They made a town within the city where it was possible to survive without ever having to speak English.

In the 1960s, the flood of Chinese from Hong Kong gave birth to the new Chinatown. This was a more westernized, more entrepreneurial breed. Greengrocers and restaurants that had only been scattered along Dundas to Spadina were soon filled in with new malls and such a diversification of businesses that what we think of as Chinatown today encompasses the area from west of Spadina to Bay Street, College to south of Dundas. And there is further evidence of all this energy at Gerrard and Broadview, and Sheppard and Midland in Scarborough.

Rituals are what make the main Chinatown so fascinating. Saturdays and Sundays are the days when everybody in the community, no matter where they live or work, comes downtown to shop, to socialize, to eat good food. Chinese restaurants in other parts of the city close up. Their owners are down on Dundas having a good time with family and friends. One businessman estimates that at least two million dollars of business goes on every Sunday in the grocery stores, fish and meat markets, the bakeries, herbalists, book, clothing, craft stores, and the more than one hundred restaurants. Among those restaurants are some of the finest in the city. The cooking is as varied as the country itself: from Cantonese, to Hunan, to the currently popular Szechuan, almost every province of China is represented here in Toronto.

（Opposite page) As the Chinese
community grew in the Dundas and
Spadina area, its members bought up
the houses in the surrounding streets.
Some of them became clubs and
associations as owners moved away to
live in other parts of Toronto.

(Above) One of the tests of any of the
over four hundred Chinese restaurants
that are liberally sprinkled throughout
Toronto is to see whether Chinese
people eat there.

The city bestowed official recognition on Chinatown's unique
character when it erected the first street signs in both English and
Chinese. Even the telephone booths were decorated to look like
mini-pagodas. In 1977, the Sunday customs were also taken into
account. The Blue Laws that demand Sunday closing for all but
tourist areas were lifted. Chinatown does not, however, function
for the sake of tourists. Its purpose is to keep this resonant community alive and its citizens in touch with each other.

(*Previous pages*) This is the new Chinatown. It almost feels like Hong Kong with such a crowded jumble of businesses located all along Dundas Street. The Chinese, especially those who do come from Hong Kong, love the busy street life.

(*Above*) This Chinese court was the first shopping mall in the Chinatown area. It is still the most elaborate. On Sundays it is crowded. This is the day when all generations socialize, eat dim sum and catch up with the local news.

(*Opposite page*) There are five Chinese newspapers published for distribution in the community. The Chinese also have their own advertising agencies and stock brokers.

# CABBAGETOWN

Gerrard Street during the low period of Cabbagetown's history. The area then as now was filled with alleys and little side streets that are any child's timeless playground.

(*Opposite page*) The old corner stores that proliferated throughout the neighbourhood have gone through dramatic transformations. One is now an ice cream parlour, others have become antique stores. This store has been spruced up tastefully and still functions as a place not only to shop but to meet friends and neighbours who live in the streets around it.

Cabbagetown is now synonymous with domestic chic: sandblasted brick, wrought iron fences, fresh paint trim. Cabbagetown used to be synonymous with North America's largest Anglo-Saxon slum. A place to escape from. Now it is a place to return to.

It was settled in the 1880s by Irish fleeing the potato famine. They planted cabbages in their front yards determined never to starve again. It grew into a solid stable working-class neighbourhood during this century. Even so, in the 1960s city planners decided to impose 20th century urban renewal on this very 19th century area. They tore down hundreds of houses to make room for highrises.

By the late 1960s, however, middle-class professional people began to recognize that it was more fun to live downtown than in the suburbs. The venturesome moved in, enlisting the aid of long-time residents to keep the area they loved intact and humane. Once stabilized, Cabbagetown flourished. It has all the fundamental elements to maintain itself as an independent neighbourhood: a high street, Parliament Street, with its centre of commerce plus specialty shops, galleries and restaurants. Scattered through the back streets there are corner stores and even an ice cream parlor. People from every walk of life live side by side. In late summer they celebrate their neighbourhood: the Cabbagetown Cultural Festival. The district becomes a giant yard sale, an open house with a veritable cornucopia of good food and music for two days.

The natural boundaries of Cabbagetown emerged in the 1830s: St. James Cemetery to the north, Don Valley to the east, Parliament on the west and Gerrard to the south. Historically it was part of a large park reserve established in 1790. Early developers built their grand homes on estate corners with an eye to further land division. You can see the mansions carefully situated throughout the area. The backyards and lawns of these early estates are now filled in with tall, elegant row houses that date from 1875, and narrow workers' cottages in such bewildering variety of domestic architecture it makes the district one of the most captivating in the city. There's everything here from Victorian Gothic to Greek Revival. From Toronto's first low-cost housing project (1913) to the original farm houses.

A scrubbed-up look has revived this once-decaying neighbourhood. It now has an elegance that the original inhabitants would have envied – and cheered.

(*Opposite page above*) The workers'
cottages that dot the streets looked like
this before the renovators took over
in the late 1960s. They had a neat cosy
quality to them; today few have been
left in their original state.

(*Opposite page below*) This small
square at Parliament and Gerrard is
set against the converted mansard-
roofed houses that fill the streets of
downtown Toronto. Many are still in
the process of being converted from
crowded rooming houses to flats,
shops and cafes.

(*Above*) This house, built in the 1880s,
is one of the most interesting in
Cabbagetown. The strange but
fascinating brick carving shows the
whimsical nature of domestic
architecture at that time. The house
has been lovingly restored and its
owner has added a further element of
fantasy by painting it white, and
emphasizing the gingerbread trim. It
stands apart from the sandblasted brick
which is the area's usual trademark.

(*Opposite page*) Row houses such as these filled in the spaces around the area's original grand estates. The three-storey gabled brick houses were once inhabited by tenants. Now they have been returned to single-family dwellings. Each one reflects its owner's taste, giving the area its distinct character.

(*Above*) The charm of these lovely 19th-century cottages has not been lost in the restoration. The owners here have worked together to keep the integrity of the simple little houses intact.

# PARKDALE

Building the Lansdowne Park Line in 1916. In those days, the streetcar tracks were put down using horse and buggy. This line made Parkdale accessible, and it became the playground of Toronto.

(*Opposite page*) Roncesvalles Avenue at the eastern edge of Parkdale has strong Polish and Ukrainian roots. They give a definite character to their own part of the neighbourhood. The street is crammed with shops like this that serve both as a deli and greengrocer.

Parkdale was celebrated, in the very distant past, as the only area of Toronto that was a true visual paradise. In the 1970s it was denigrated as "the dumping ground of Toronto". Today it is a combination of magnificent old houses saved from ruin, teeming highrises, crowded rooming houses and humble single family dwellings.

South Parkdale, the envy of all Toronto in the 19th century, is nothing more than expressways and railroad tracks now – a legacy of the 1950s boom years. The area we know today as Parkdale is to the north of Queen down to the Gardiner Expressway, Dufferin to Roncesvalles in the West. It's a neighbourhood struggling to regain its dignity and, on the whole, succeeding against improbable odds.

From 1879 to 1889, Parkdale was a separate village containing large rambling houses with huge verandahs. Its main streets swept down to the lake where the most impressive homes were set on wide lawns and terraces under huge elm trees.

A referendum to join the city in 1879 drew such a reaction from the citizenry that they took to the streets. They wanted to preserve what they had: the water was cleaner out here, the air sweeter and cooler because of its proximity to the lake. Despite strong local resistance, they lost to City Hall pressure in 1888.

People had been commuting by railway to the new houses west of Dufferin at the time they were annexed a year later. When the streetcar was introduced along Queen in 1890, Parkdale became even more accessible. It was no longer an elite suburb, it was the playground of Toronto. There was a boardwalk, beaches, bathing pavilions and dance halls. In 1920, Sunnyside was built at the beach. But this "Riviera of the Poor Man" was destroyed in 1950 when the expressway was pushed through.

After World War II there was a vast influx of immigrants of every variety. This is where you find a real cultural mosaic: Filipinos, Sikhs, Czechs, Greeks, Portuguese, West Indians and Germans all flocked out here because the rents were affordable, the houses solid. Each group made bits of Parkdale their own.

During the 1970s, heated debates were fought in the beleaguered area as it had then become. The district had a reputation as a place of last resort. This did not discourage young people who saw the crumpled glory of those great old houses. Working with their more established neighbours, they organized associations and fought against the general decay in morale.

(*Above*) Renovations are beginning to make an impact on the neighbourhood. Mews such as Melbourne Place have been restored meticulously.

(*Opposite page above*) Parkdale has been a stop-gap area for those on the way up, or down. Queen Street cordiality is a normal part of the street.

(*Opposite page below*) The grim highrise apartment buildings along Jameson Avenue replaced fine old 19th century houses. But children who fill the buildings don't seem to mind as they play blissfully together here.

One of their major projects, Centennial Square, at Queen and Cowan has given them a focus and the uplift they needed. It is a village centre, brick-paved with benches, planting boxes and historical street lamps. In 1979 when Parkdale celebrated its one hundredth anniversary, 20,000 jubilant people showed up. Parkdale is still fluid, still non-exclusive. It is the gutsiest of all Toronto neighbourhoods.

(*Opposite page*) The ethnic mix of Parkdale involves just about every group that immigrated to Canada in the 20th century. It is a true reflection of the city's multicultural mosaic.

(*Above*) When Parkdale celebrated its 100th anniversary in 1978, Centennial Square was one of the major new neighbourhood projects with its brick paving, planters and benches. With the community centre perched at the edge, the Square is now a central meeting place.

# HIGH PARK

A busy day for Sunday motorists in High Park, 1912. Ladies and gentlemen were apparently allowed to leave their cars anywhere while they took a leisurely stroll around the park.

(*Opposite page*) Throughout the park's 399 acres there is ample opportunity for pleasing every kind of need for pastoral retreat. Not far from this quiet bench there are large sculptures, a small zoo and Colborne Lodge. This was the original home of John Howard who donated most of the park land to the city in 1876.

High Park began with architect John Howard. He built his home, Colborne Lodge (named after an early patron), in the middle of the most beautiful forest in the environs of York, in 1837. He was so enchanted by the 165-acre lot he owned that he decided, in 1873, to deed 120 acres of it to the city for a public park. Howard, who was the architect of the Don Jail (1836) and laid out the grounds for Osgoode Hall and St. James Cemetery, was also a naturalist. He envisioned the park as both a recreation area and a natural preserve for birds, fish and plants of all kinds. This park, he insisted, was not to be named after himself – a rare instance of diffidence in Toronto benefactors. He wanted it to be called High Park because of its dazzling view of Lake Ontario. When he died, in 1890, he left another forty-five acres and Colborne Lodge to the city.

Since the days when the Grenadier Guards, on leave from Fort York, hunted and fished on the pond named after them, many more acres have been added to the park. Today it comprises 399 acres. It is still a place to walk through untouched bush, to listen to band concerts or watch theatre in the open air.

High Park Avenue, north of Bloor, was designed to be one of the major avenues of the west end. It is four lanes wide with a boulevard shaded by giant maple trees. Grand old houses are set well off the street harking back to Howard's more elegant era.

In the mid-1960s, when the east-west subway was being built, it was decided that the area from Keele to Roncesvalles should be zoned high density. Developers moved in quickly to raze the area for highrises. But neighbourhood committees were organized by 1971 and they fought back. They didn't win the battle completely. Apartment buildings tower awkwardly among the nice old houses north of Bloor. But the line was held at Gothic Avenue.

The east end of the area, around Roncesvalles, is a complete contrast to the parkside district. It was the point of entry for Poles and Ukrainians who came into the city in the early part of this century. Copernicus Lodge, a home for seniors of Polish extraction, was built on Roncesvalles amid the crowded delis and restaurants that still exude the exciting flavour of their European background.

Closer to the park, south of Bloor, a solid Anglo area still survives in modest well-kept houses on neatly treed streets. Even renovators have barely made a dent. There are ten churches here. With active and loyal congregations, they have followed their leaders in

keeping Bloor Street free of liquor in public places from Indian Road right out to Jane Street. John Howard would approve. He made it a provision of his will in perpetuity that no spirits could be served in High Park. His influence carries on.

High Park neighbourhood is a curious mixture of ethnic and staid Anglo-Saxon. It is one of the loveliest parts of the city. Yet it manifests the conflict between the strait-laced temperance past of Toronto, and the much more liberal and sunny European present.

(*Opposite page*) This charming French cafe with its art nouveau decor is a contrast to the other High Park area restaurants which lean heavily to Ukrainian and Polish food.

(*Above*) Grenadier Pond looking towards the heights of Swansea. There is a park legend that a troop of Grenadier Guards was marching across the pond in winter and perished when the ice gave way under them. The pond was actually named for the guards because they used to come out here to hunt and fish during the early 1800s.

(*Opposite page*) In the 19th century, High Park Avenue was designed to be the show-case street of the west end. This house reflects that ambition. It is a graceful mixture of styles the Victorians loved so well: from the slender Greek columns of the porch to the tower that repeats the shingles of the arches below, and to the Romanesque windows of the first floor.

(*Above*) Humberside Collegiate is a huge school happily situated on gently rolling hills. It is also a very good school. In the days before nearby Swansea was incorporated by the city, parents paid to have their children enrolled here.

(*Overleaf*) There are several tranquil ponds in High Park such as this one. They are stocked with a variety of exotic fish and indigenous plants.

# ROSEDALE

The Rosedale ravine was a well-used and much beloved public place as far back as the turn of the century when this photograph was taken.

(*Opposite page*) The ravines and public walking spaces through Rosedale cover more than two hundred acres. Most of them can be reached by public transportation. They are seemingly isolated from the city, yet close enough to the bridges and large buildings that stalk this quiet enclave.

Rosedale was Toronto's first suburb. It was destined for the rich, protected as it is by ravines. It is a place where each house is its owner's castle, even if it does sit on a small lot. It is swathed in trees, four thousand of them, that have been preserved for over a hundred years. No other city in North America has been able to maintain such a gracious residential neighbourhood so close to the heart of the city.

It is bounded by Yonge Street to the Don Valley in the east, Bloor Street to the railroad tracks in the north. Giant homes on curving streets give this locality a settled sense of being almost ancient.

There is no corner store in Rosedale. That was ruled out in 1905. One small street, Summerhill Avenue, was left to service the whole area – a grocery store, hair dresser, and meat market are still there – but so obscure only locals could possibly find them.

The district was touched with gold almost from its beginning. Mrs. Simcoe made her country cottage at Castle Frank and moving north became fashionable in the 1800s. When Colonel William Botsford Jarvis built his estate on part of his two-hundred-acre lot in 1874, the Establishment felt free to follow north away from the dust and congestion of the city. Mary Jarvis was so enchanted by the profusion of wild roses on their property she named it Rosedale. By 1890, Sir Donald Macpherson had bought the estate, started subdividing it with meandering streets and by 1900 there were at least eighty mansions.

The spirit of Rosedale is determined. Wartime housing shortages turned old mansions into rooming houses. That opened the way for developers who, conforming to local by-laws for a three-storey limit, constructed apartment buildings that spilled down the ravine lots they had picked up. It also made living in an apartment quite all right – if it was in Rosedale. Residents plagued by high taxes and the huge expenses of keeping up these old mausoleums moved to have mixed use legalized: turn rambling houses into flats rather than have them destroyed. This attracted young families back into the area in the 70s. It kept original family houses intact and safe from "progress" and by 1979 when a developer destroyed a ninety-three-year-old house for townhouse development, the neighbours turned out to jeer.

This early suburb pioneered such progressive measures as putting hydro wires underground more than sixty years ago.

Mansions that were torn down often evolved into public places. Chorley Park is one example. The tradition goes back to 1924 when the Osler estate, all thirteen acres, was turned over to the city. It is now Craigleigh Gardens, a public park, alas without the original house.

Rosedale, in spite of its reputation, is not and probably never has been stuffy. It encompasses miles of walking lands, is filled with theatre folk and students as well as the old families. Not merely a preserve of grandeur, Rosedale has retained a neighbour-liness that has kept this special part of the city very much alive.

(*Opposite page*) When most people think of Rosedale they have something like this grand manor in mind. Even though this house is built on a mansion-like scale, it sits on a relatively small lot. This is peculiar to all parts of Toronto and not just Rosedale.

(*Above*) Brick fences are unusual in Toronto. This fine old one not only affords the owners privacy, it also adds an attractive element to the street.

(*Opposite page*) This front porch is a charming contradiction that is almost typical of Toronto. The refined proportions of the Georgian doorway and the interesting fan light over it are somewhat trivialized by a later addition of incongruous iron grillwork.

(*Above*) Rosedale architecture is as varied as the people who live there. It can be loosely described as eclectic. Though much of the architecture is mixed, grand old houses such as this one give an overall charm to the neighbourhood.

Someone once pointed out that Toronto is a city built in a forest. The streets of Rosedale with their leafy bowers and generous parks, in this case Craigleigh Gardens, prove the point.

# THE ISLANDS/ HARBOURFRONT

Hanlan's Point in 1907 shows the handsome hotel that was a place of merry making from the 1890s until it burned down early in this century. It was never replaced. During its heyday, Ned Hanlan, the World Champion Oarsman was its proprietor.

(*Opposite page*) The string of islands is linked by attractive little bridges such as this one. The waterways that run through the islands are perfect for the weekend canoeist in summer, and for skaters in winter.

Ward's Island is a microcosm of all Toronto neighbourhoods. It began by chance and has survived for almost six generations. In Ward's case, however, the neighbourhood sits on public land – a park that the Metropolitan Government now wants back. Though the community takes up less than three per cent of that park, it has been embroiled in this fight for survival since the 1950s.

The Islanders, bound as they are by exigencies of weather, ferry schedules and the invasion of casual tourists each weekend, are a particularly hardy breed. They have been galvanized by creative resistance, endless court battles and appeals. Their fate, tenuous all these years, is also a part of what makes them a neighbourhood. They endure through a sense of obduracy and knowing they add to, rather than subtract from, a conventional park.

The first real home on the islands was Governor General Lord Sydenham's summer residence in 1839. That was when the harbour was the main focus of both commerce and recreation for the city. By the 1840s, there were hotels, bandstands, boardwalks, dance pavilions and gingerbread-encrusted cottages of astonishing beauty. On Ward's Island, tents sprang up on rented lots to be replaced by permanent cottages in the 1930s. During the war-time housing shortage, 10,000 people lived on the Island.

The islands, three and a half miles long, loosely strung together, contain beaches, rides, marinas and the yacht clubs whose unchallenged space is more than twice that of the residents.

Ironically Ward's looks across the water to the most dramatic view of the city and to Harbourfront. After decades of indecision (since 1912), the lakefront, made inaccessible by acres of roads and railway lines, is finally being returned to people. The change began in the 1970s with retrieved park space, warehouses converted into galleries and theatres, and the creation of superb playgrounds for children. The waterfront has evolved into a giant community centre.

What Harbourfront did not have until recently was a real sense of neighbourhood. This changed in 1983 with the opening of Queen's Quay Terminal. The magnificent renovation not only boasts shops, restaurants and theatres, it also offers condominiums. This is the touchstone for all the new buildings planned for construction in the next few years. And these new residences won't be just for those who can afford the yachts bobbing about in the marinas. The plan is for mixed housing – from apartments to sleek town-

houses – to attract not only the well-to-do but also people for the non-profit housing units owned by the city. Along with these buildings there will be museums, parks, shops and office buildings. In a few years this will be the real neighbourhood of the waterfront.

Toronto is being enhanced in reclaiming its right to Lake Ontario. The new development of Harbourfront and the survival of Ward's Island community will give this most important area of the city the focus it once had in the 19th century.

For years after Hanlan's Hotel burned down and the cottages were razed to make room for parkland on the Point, this island was occupied mainly by grass, beaches and tennis courts. Now there is an attractive outdoor cafe near the ferry landing. It offers a breathtaking view of the city.

(*Above*) The ferries travel to three main points on the islands: Ward's, Centre and Hanlan's Point. The only crowding is on Centre Island in the summer, where there are amusement rides, a children's farm, fast food outlets and organized picnic grounds. Even without an island destination, these old ferries are worth a ride in themselves.

(*Overleaf*) Attractive little cottages like these make up part of the Ward's Island community. They cover some nineteen acres on public parkland. Islanders are a welcoming lot. In winter, they post notices for cross-country skiers as to who's holding open house.

(*Opposite page*) In the late 1960s, a flock of Canada Geese stopped off at the Islands for a rest on their way north. They liked it so much, they stayed. The size of the flock has increased considerably and they can sometimes be a hazard for the small planes at the Island Airport, but most visitors get along well with them.

(*Above*) Thousands of people show up on weekends for the outdoor antique and flea market at Harbourfront. It brings together professional dealers and amateurs who scour yard sales and bring the loot down here for re-sale.

(*Overleaf*) This is perhaps Canada's most ambitious warehouse renovation. The developer and architect had a sensitive approach to this grand old building. They kept art deco details, opened up the ground floor for restaurants with a lake view, and made the interior mall the best indoor public space in town.

# KENSINGTON

The corner of College and Spadina, an uncommonly wide street of 132 feet. It had only begun to develop as a commercial area when this photograph was taken in 1912.

(*Opposite page*) The market has its characters. Some come in costume and some don't. The sign behind the clown suggests the presence of the most recent arrivals in the district–the Vietnamese.

Kensington has evolved from a turn-of-the-century Jewish ghetto into a captivating market-centred neighbourhood. Everything is compact: from the gaudy Portuguese hardware store on Denison Square to the endless stalls of fruit, vegetables, dried beans, fish and cheese, to the New Wave clothing stores in New Kensington. In this cramped space are the Jewish residents, who've lived there for generations, the Portuguese who've slowly taken over in the past thirty years, the more recently arrived West Indians, Boat People and the young whose tastes run more to tofu and brown rice than a freshly butchered chicken.

The survival of this riotously cheerful area is somewhat of a miracle. There's always someone around who wants to clean it up: live chickens and ducks in cages became a target in 1982; earlier, in 1966, a plan was proposed to tear down the whole place for urban renewal. But its citizens have been consistently stubborn. Despite outside pressure, they have insisted on a more humane approach to what they know is one of the most valuable historical neighbourhoods in Toronto.

Kensington is bounded by Bathurst and Spadina, Dundas and College. The main streets of the market include Augusta, Baldwin and Kensington Avenue. Every day is a festival of noise, movement and an extraordinary mixture of smells, but on weekends it reaches a fever pitch of activity.

The area was originally a park lot given to Captain John Denison in 1815. He built his house, Belle Vue, the same year (Kiever Synagogue now stands on the site). His beautiful view was of the sweeping lawns that looked north. They are evident today in the uncharacteristically wide setback of the houses along what is now Bellevue Avenue. But in the 1850s and 60s, the land was subdivided so many times, the pattern of closely built narrow houses was established.

The first immigrants to move in were of British stock. By 1900, they had moved away making room for newly arrived Jews from central and southern Europe. The Jewish merchants started off with the ubiquitous hand-carts which later came to rest permanently on their tiny lawns. Kensington then became known, appropriately, as the Jewish Market. By the 1930s, they were well-established and had built two synagogues, Kiever in 1925 and Minsker in 1930. Hungarians and Italians arrived but no group had so much influence as the influx of Portuguese in the 1950s.

Today they make up half of the population. Houses are painted bright colours, gilt is everywhere, Fado music blares from furniture stores. The most recent habitués of the market are the New Wavers. Baldwin Street and Kensington Avenue now sport such shops as Parade and Courage My Love, XOX Postcards and lively spots like Tiger's Coconut Grove, with its magnetic reggae beat that attracts the large West Indian community to the south of Dundas. The next groups to join the fray can be seen among the Korean food stalls and the Vietnamese restaurants.

Kensington, in its own matchless style, manages to combine the most vivid traditional aspects of the old world with survival in a cold climate. And it has not lost one bit of vitality in doing it.

(*Above*) In some ways Kensington resembles a bazaar, with stalls like this one selling all manner of religious items, plaster fruit and animals, and gilt ornaments.

(*Opposite page*) Outsiders have been trying for years to get rid of the chickens, rabbits and ducks kept in cages until bought and slaughtered. So far they've been unsuccessful, much to the customers' gastronomic satisfaction.

(*Opposite page*) Augusta and Nassau Streets are at the heart of the market. In the old days haggling used to be a common practice. Though this is no longer the custom, people still come for fresh food bargains.

(*Above*) The neat and brightly painted houses make delightful streetscapes throughout Kensington. Many of them, like this house, have religious icons and plaster ornaments on their lawns.

(*Above*) A Portuguese fish market displaying all its finny wares. The merchants shout out the virtues of the catch and, if you believe them, there is no fresher fish available–anywhere.

(*Opposite page*) Neighbours talking over the front fence are part of the Kensington hotline. In this case, the local news is passed on in Portuguese. The brightly coloured houses and the stacks of wooden grape boxes are part of the ambiance of Kensington.

# BLOOR WEST VILLAGE/ SWANSEA

The outer reaches of Bloor Street West back in 1914. In spite of the wretched condition of the roads, mansions had been built in Swansea overlooking the Humber River and the valleys in the district.

(*Opposite page*) One of the most remarkable changes in the west end was the improvement of Bloor Street West. The tidy wide streets, trees and delightful display of wares, make it one of the most pleasant places to shop in the city. The clowns here are part of the annual village festival.

Bloor West Village, at Jane and Bloor, almost died when Toronto's east-west subway opened in 1966. Shoppers deserted the old stores in favour of downtown shopping. Local businessmen were devastated and almost ready to close down when they decided they could revitalize their own district. They dug into their own pockets (by raising business taxes) to widen the street, install neat brick sidewalks, and plant trees strung with fairy-lights that burned all night. The locals made a new streetscape and named it Bloor West Village.

The neighbours who had previously patronized the shops of Bloor West were WASP. But stores that had opened up in rapid succession reflected every wave of immigration into the area from the early part of this century: Ukrainian, Polish, Austrian, Estonian, Lithuanian, German. With the street spruced up, the cafes and shops followed suit. Meat markets, delis, bakeries and pastry shops held such an abundance of delectable goods that people came from all over the city to shop. The subway now serves the merchants well. For the neighbourhood, they were classy enough to compete with anything downtown and a lot more convenient. Business boomed. Not only did the main street appeal to the people of European extraction who live in the tidy box-like houses to the north of Bloor, but also to middle- and upper middle-class Swansea-ites.

Swansea runs from Bloor down to the Gardiner, from the Humber River over to High Park in the east. There are lavish estates on the hills overlooking the Humber. The area between those and the grandiose homes near the park was filled by white collar workers who moved into the area from the town of West Toronto Junction in the 1920s.

Swansea was incorporated as a village in 1926 and was not amalgamated by Toronto until 1966. It retained a naturally independent nature, maintaining its own services, police force and way of doing things.

Swansea's history reaches back to 1846 when a man named Mark Coe bought fifty acres of land on what is now Windermere and Ellis Avenue. The landscape, with its hills and ponds, was so similar to places in Wales Coe knew, he named it Swansea.

The area blossomed in the real estate fever that swept across the suburbs when the Grand Trunk Railway took over the Steam Belt Railway in 1892.

Everyone remembers the days of summer when lemonade stands were set up to earn spending money. Here on a hot afternoon some Swansea children wait for thirsty neighbours.

Speculators thought they'd make their fortunes once these outreaches became accessible. Unfortunately the Belt Line only ran until 1894 – and Swansea stagnated in the years following.

By 1906, Jane Street was still a wagon track and all supplies had to be brought in from Parkdale twice a week. The development of Bloor Street changed that. The lovely woods were cut down, streets were laid out. It meant rapid growth and by 1907 the first wave of immigrants moved in.

The west end of Toronto is a felicitous mix of housing styles and a charming pride of ownership. People care, a lot, about their lawns and gardens. It is a lovely place to wander through as the landscape is quite different from anywhere else in Toronto. And there is the streetscape of Bloor West Village which is so special.

In the late 19th century, Swansea was one of the choice suburban areas of Toronto. Stately mansions, like this one, were built on huge expanses of grass, overlooking the Humber River, and surrounded by opulent gardens.

(*Opposite page above*) Bloor West Village is a main street created by local ingenuity. When the opening of the subway siphoned off most of their business, the merchants re-furbished the street as well as their own shops. Today business is booming.

(*Opposite page below*) There are now twenty-four food establishments along the street such as this inviting one. Twenty-five years ago most of the patrons were Anglo-Saxon, now eighty per cent are of European background and they come from all over the city to shop for home-made delectables.

(*Above*) The winding streets of Swansea are lined with graceful houses and carefully tended gardens. The land here is hilly, a sharp contrast with the rest of the city, and very sandy. Almost a hundred years of attention have turned it into one of the lushest neighbourhoods in the city.

(*Overleaf*) Most Toronto neighbourhoods have very good playground facilities. As the children here seem to indicate even this most traditional of merry-go-rounds continues to provide endless fun.

# FOREST HILL

There wasn't much of a forest left at Avenue Road and St. Clair by 1917. When the area was developed, a local by-law was passed that required each person to plant a tree outside their home. The leafy bowered streets of today are a result of that good judgement.

(*Opposite page*) One of the most familiar signs of Forest Hill is students from the local private schools shopping in the Village. In this case, girls in Bishop Strachan uniforms pick up delicacies from the local bakery.

Forest Hill is Toronto's most exclusive area. It oozes wealth and power. It excludes development and growth. Traditionally a preserve of money, from old Establishment and Jewish families to the more recent successful entrepreneurs, it has remained insular.

What holds this purlieu together, apart from the ties of money, are clubs, religious institutions and the superb educational facilities the area offers. A famous private school for boys, Upper Canada College, moved here in 1891, another, Bishop Strachan, for girls in 1915. By 1935, with the addition of Forest Hill Collegiate and Junior High School, parents here had the best staffed public and private schools in the country. If there is one thing that will draw out all of Forest Hill it is a Home and School Meeting.

Forest Hill's most beautiful avenue, Old Forest Hill Road, was originally an Indian trail, and today it still meanders through the Village in the manner of a path through a sylvan retreat. And on this street you can now gaze on a style of domestic architecture that's often been described as Stockbroker Baronial.

The area is bounded by Bathurst on the west, to Avenue Road, from St. Clair to Eglinton in the north. It was incorporated as a village in 1924 and took its name from the summer residence of John Wickson who had a cottage of the same name in 1860. Until the name changed it was Spadina Heights. Spadina (Spad-eena to Fine Old Ontario Families) bisects the area and acts as the Village centre. There is perhaps no more compact main street in the whole city. Everyone meets at the grocer, the meat market and the haute gourmet shops. It is not unusual, either, to see limousines double-parked along the street as the drivers run errands.

There is no subdividing or rooms for rent in this prosperous ghetto. In the 30s, miles of sewers were installed and residents acquired their own hydroelectric and waterworks system. Everything, of course, ran at a profit. Private garbage collection meant you didn't have any unsightly detritus on the street. It is still picked up discreetly at the side of the house. This was a condition of Forest Hill's incorporation by the city in 1967. When small industries located at the north end of the district in 1931, the Village association passed by-laws to keep them out. Ever aware of its image, the Village council appointed a board of architects in 1936 to approve of new house designs.

The population is divided evenly between Gentile and Jewish residents. Holy Blossom Temple located on Bathurst Street in 1938

and its congregation drifted north to this most pleasant of suburbs. They settled mainly west of Spadina at that time.

The Village east of Spadina has remained totally stable. Residents have been going to Grace Church-on-the-Hill since 1912; their children attending BSS and UCC since the turn of the century. The houses reflect continuity with the past as evidenced in the manorial style leaning toward Victorian Gothic.

Forest Hill with its *nouveau* energy has a quality uniquely its own. It is very subtle and, as you would expect, this is the most tranquil of all Toronto neighbourhoods.

(*Above*) The huge limestone mansions of Forest Hill, built with fabulous materials in a variety of architectural styles, date from the turn of the century to the 1920s.

(*Opposite page*) Upper Canada College, founded in 1829, moved from King Street to Lonsdale and Avenue Road in 1891. The attractive buildings and the shimmering greensward that surrounds them host young men engaged in learning and sports.

Grace Church-on-the-Hill was
established in Forest Hill in 1912. Its
distinctive architecture and the use of
limestone is reflected in many of the
stately homes in the area.

Lovely details are a hallmark of the
domestic architecture in Forest Hill.
This simple Georgian door with
handsome pediment is an example of
that careful attention.

The main street of Forest Hill is
Spadina Avenue and its central
point is at Lonsdale. Many of the
specialty stores, the hardware, grocery
and meat market have been there
since the Village's incorporation in
the 1920s.

A sunny day in Amsterdam Park,
named after Toronto's twin city. The
fountain in the background is a replica
of one in The Hague. This charming
park at Avenue Road and St. Clair is
much beloved by the local residents.

# QUEEN STREET WEST

This is Queen Street back in 1911. The trolley had been installed, but a great deal of commerce went on with horse and wagon.

(*Opposite page*) Peter Pan Lunch established Queen Street chic. A group of counterculture entrepreneurs bought it in 1976. Restored to the original 1920s feeling with panache and little money, it was an instant hit with the street regulars and it also became a magnet for tourists from every part of the city.

At first inspection it looks intimidating: the parade of New Wave youth along the rialto of Queen Street. But the garish clothes and the unisex Mohawk haircuts disguise the most benign of young people.

Queen Street is full of surprises. At one corner stalls of hand-decorated shirts and funky artifacts can appear out of nowhere. A chapati cart turns up, and its owners provide, as well as food, chairs for patrons to sit on while they eat and watch a movie being screened on the wall of a building by a parking lot. This is an area of travelling parties and happenings, of after-hours clubs and speakeasies. Queen Street, this tribe of young people will tell you, is an attitude. It welcomes observers and participants alike.

In the late 60s, American draft dodgers discovered spacious lofts in the crumbling local warehouses. To them, the area recalled SoHo in New York. In the early 70s, artists-cum-entrepreneurs moved in to create respectable studio and living spaces in abandoned factories. It was, for some, as far away as they could get and still be in Toronto. They now live comfortably next to the Poles, the Ukrainians, the Russian and Slavic Jews who had immigrated at the turn of the century, many of whom ended up working in the sweat shops along Spadina.

It was those immigrants who, as they prospered, bought the buildings along Queen, opened second-hand furniture and junk shops, clothing jobbers, delis and restaurants where pirogies are still king. The owners of these buildings now sleep in their suburban dream homes, but they still come down here to work. The accommodating nature of the area from Bathurst to University, King to Dundas hosts these original eccentrics and the more recently arrived – the artists, photographers, musicians – that have in some measure always been a part of the ambiance of Queen Street.

The origins of the area go back to 1800 when the land was divided in one-hundred-acre lots and handed out to military colleagues of Governor John Graves Simcoe. They became the wealthy colonial aristocracy. The grandeur of those times remains in Grange House which today stands on the grounds of the Art Gallery of Ontario.

As lots were sold off in the 19th century, smaller houses filled in the spaces. Then came the factories and warehouses. The poorer immigrants stayed behind as the Annex and other suburbs became fashionable for those who could afford it.

Queen Street was once the exclusive home of discount stores and jobbers. They exist side by side with the boutiques, bookstores and galleries that are the hallmark of the street today.

Once known as the Lower Ward, the area has endured hard times. But now Queen Street chi-chi has made its mark. It has become a major restaurant area, pubs abound and Grange Park has been revitalized as a meeting place. There is even a new housing development on Soho Street that reflects its splendid past. And there are always the strange and wonderful street people to give an inimitable blend of vitality and character.

(*Above*) The new townhouses in what is now called Old Soho have been designed to fit into the locale off Soho Street. They have been built on the site of the original farm, Petersfield, owned by Peter Russell in the 1790s.

(*Overleaf*) The Riv, as the Rivoli Restaurant is called, is the central hangout for the tribe that collects along Queen Street. Good cheap food, music that ranges from ear-shattering new wave to Bach, and a crowd that might include the moms and dads from the suburbs visiting their kids, are all part of this lively scene.

The warm brick facades of the stores
along the street have, in a lot of cases,
been restored with good bookstores
and galleries. Over them live a mix of
artists, students from nearby Ontario
College of Art and young people in
the busy process of finding themselves.

Queen Street is to new wave in the 80s
what Yorkville was to hippies in the
60s. The new wavers also buy their
clothes here. Anything that can be
recycled will be: fashion is not
necessarily a matter of good taste.
Young people come from all over to
find the latest in trendy garb.

# ST. LAWRENCE/ DOWNTOWN CORE

In 1844, St. Lawrence Market was Toronto's first City Hall. By 1890, it had become the farmer's market. In 1919, when this shot was taken, it looked pretty much like it does today– except for the wagons.

(*Opposite page*) This traditional view up the Bay Street business corridor to old City Hall warms the hearts of all Torontonians. The massive 1890s building designed by E. J. Lennox was the result of an international architectural competition.

St. Lawrence is a rare and daring neighbourhood project. It needed the co-operation of three levels of government. It contains middle-class rental, condominiums, co-operatives and subsidized housing. This is a created neighbourhood. It is an attempt to replicate the 19th-century Toronto that worked so well. The buildings are low in scale: entrances open onto streets which have been kept short with many intersections. The Esplanade which bisects the area is not only its main street, but also a beautifully integrated park. The district covers Yonge to Parliament, Front St. to the railway tracks.

Everyday services such as dry cleaners and corner stores have moved into an area already rich in restaurants, galleries, theatres and churches. People can sit on their porches and balconies and watch the sun set. Because it is an instant neighbourhood without a history, the people who live there have a particular camaraderie in building one from scratch.

And yet nearby there are almost eighty historical buildings. Luxury condominiums which now fill the former wasteland of parking lots on Market Square are constructed of yellow brick to blend with St. Lawrence Hall (1850). The park surrounding St. James (1853) has a music pavilion and in the evening the cathedral bells ring out the day.

In Old York, further east and up to King Street, there are fine examples of warehouse architecture which St. Lawrence has been modelled after. Workmen's cottages have been restored; and with all this activity, there's been a slow up-grading of shops along King Street.

Front Street in the downtown core was once at the water's edge. Landfill over the centuries has placed it half a mile away. Once it was a forgotten street, shabby with neglect. Now it has re-emerged. There has been a dramatic turnaround in respect for what was the original town. Instead of tearing down old inconvenient buildings, the city in the late 1960s started restoring and re-structuring what already existed.

The cityscape of monolithic edifices is now softened by the presence of buildings such as the Flat Iron Gooderham (1892), the old Bank of Montreal (1885); the new and old city halls at Queen and Bay are a vivid contrast in the style of two centuries. The Eaton Centre, that most hi-tech of shopping malls, has Holy Trinity Church (1847) nestled in beside it comfortably.

(*Previous pages*) The south market draws customers any day of the week. It has been taken over from the farmers (they ply their trade in the north market on Saturdays only) and has been a permanent fixture for many decades. Everything from fish and cheese to fruit and nuts is available.

These stone consciences challenge the new. They say you must do better, or at least as well. The power that emanates from the money centre of the nation is kept in perspective by the presence of these magnificent old buildings. They draw us back to our roots, and explain why people from all over the world were inspired to stay in what was then a marshy hinterland. Because of its care and respect for neighbourhoods, Toronto today is one of the loveliest and most humane cities in North America.

(*Opposite page*) It's hard to believe that during the 1970s anyone would have considered pulling down this magnificent building. Union Station was threatened when passenger railway service became unprofitable, but a fiercely resistant citizens' committee helped save it. Today, with new commuter services in operation, it is busier than ever.

(*Above*) Where you work is also part of your neighbourhood. This plaza behind the Commerce Court with fountain and trees is a welcome respite from the usual windswept open spaces of the giant downtown complexes. The original 1930s building gives this space a more humane and welcoming atmosphere.

This row of handsomely restored
buildings would be comfortable in any
European city. They were once the
factories and warehouses of the 1880s
when Front Street was on the
waterfront.

St. Lawrence Neighbourhood means there is activity all the time in the downtown core. This brave experiment in urban living has been one of the great successes of town planners in the 1980s.

# PHOTOGRAPH CREDITS

**Nir Baraket**
Pages 12, 13, 44, 48, 70, 74, 75, 88, 92

**Steve Behal**
Pages 86-87

**Ian Crysler**
Pages 53, 73, 109

**Gera Dillon**
Pages 2, 6, 60, 68-69, 112

**Ken Elliott**
Page 38

**Linda Mair**
Pages 37, 59 (bottom), 61, 65, 66, 67, 96, 98, 100 (top and bottom), 101, 104, 107, 110

**Alain Masson**
Pages 49, 58, 59 (top), 94, 95

**Larry Morse**
Pages 10, 39, 45, 46-47, 56, 72, 91, 111, 119

**John O'Brien**
Pages 80, 85, 126

**Richard Pierre**
Pages 34, 36, 40-41, 120, 124, 125

**Roberto Portolese**
Pages 26, 28-29, 30, 31, 32, 33

**Barry Ranford**
Pages 81, 82-83

**Fiona Spalding-Smith**
Pages 16, 122-123, 127

**John de Visser**
Pages 7, 14-15, 17, 18, 20-21, 52 (top and bottom), 54, 78, 84, 93

**Ron Watts**
Pages 22, 23, 24, 25, 62, 64, 76-77, 90, 99, 102-103

**John Williamson**
Pages 42, 50, 55, 106, 108, 114, 115, 116-117, 118

**Courtesy of the City of Toronto Public Archives:**
Pages 11, 19, 27, 35, 43, 51, 57, 63, 71, 79, 89, 97, 105, 113, 121.